EVERYBODY'S DOING IT!

EVERYBODY'S DOING IT!

Jere D. Patzer

REVIEW AND HERALD PUBLISHING ASSOCIATION
Washington, DC 20039-0555
Hagerstown, MD 21740

This book was
Edited by Gerald Wheeler
Designed by Dennis Ferree

Type set: 10/11 Palatino Roman

Texts credited to Phillips are from J. B. Phillips: *The New Testament in Modern English*, Revised Edition. © J. B. Phillips 1958, 1960, 1972. Used by permission of Macmillan Publishing Co., Inc.
Texts credited to RSV are from the Revised Standard Version of the Bible, copyrighted 1946, 1952 © 1971, 1973.

Printed in U.S.A.

Library of Congress Cataloging in Publication Data

Patzer, Jere.
  Everybody's doing it!

  1. Christian ethics—Seventh-day Adventist authors.
I. Title.
BJ1251.P35   1986   241'.046732   86-3199

ISBN 0-8280-0323-8

Recently researchers conducted an experiment to determine what made fish want to swim together in what we call schools. The scientists found that a fish has a line of special movement sensors alongside its head and body. This lateral line system, as biologists call it, enables a group of fish to swim in a well-schooled manner.

Not satisfied with leaving it at that, the scientists decided to disconnect surgically that part of the fish's anatomy and study the results. Then they placed the poor little fish back into the observation tank with the rest of his buddies. No longer having any desire to be with the other fish, our little convalescing fish swam off to the other end of the tank.

For a while his friends ignored him, but eventually they swam to the other end of the tank to see what the great attraction was there. And what do you suppose happened? Sure enough, they began following him. Hey, a new leader (despite the fact that part of his brain was disconnected)! Now, this rather humorous behavior is not unique to just fish.

My father, who grew up on the plains of North Dakota, has told me that for entertainment they used to trick the sheep on their farm. As he and his friends would herd their flocks from one pasture to the next, the animals would have

EVERYBODY'S DOING IT!

to go through a gate. The boys, however, would hold a stick across the opening to block their progress.

Now, sheep aren't known to be terribly intelligent, but even they could see that the only way to get to where they wanted to go was to jump over the stick. So they would—the first sheep, the second, the third, and so on. Then the boys would drop the stick, and what do you suppose sheep number 10 would do? If the first nine sheep jumped, there must be something there, so sheep numbers 10 and 11 and 12 . . . and sheep number 99 and number 100 all would jump. Why? Because all the other sheep had!

People, Too!

Now, it's funny when it happens to animals, but unfortunately, it doesn't stop there. People respond the same way. Psychologists (taking their cue from the animal kingdom) call it the herd instinct. Youth leaders call it peer pressure. And you and I know it as that certain something inside all of us that says, I'll do almost anything to be accepted by my friends. I'll do just about anything not to appear different or strange.

What's amazing is that this phenomenon starts at a very young age. Suppose my little son comes in and says, "Daddy, I want a bicycle."

"Why, Troy?"

"Because Darin has one and Dennis has one and Eric does too. Everybody's got one!"

Then boys think they need a motorcycle—then a car. For girls, it's wearing certain hairstyles or designer jeans. In time they must go to a certain college, get married, and have a family and . . . Just about the time one would think a person would grow out of this, he starts all over again with his own children—putting them in certain clothes, giving them gymnastic lessons, letting them do whatever every-

EVERYBODY'S DOING IT!

body else's children are doing because "certainly we wouldn't want our children to be different!"

Even Adults

Now, just because others are doing something doesn't make it wrong. Many people jog for their health or go to church for their spiritual growth. That's not bad—that's good! We're talking here about negative social behavior that can range from smoking or drinking in order to be accepted, to joining a cult because your friends have.

When I attended graduate school in Michigan I was fortunate enough to live on a lake where I spent many enjoyable hours waterskiing—a great diversion from studying. Frequently a boat enthusiast who lived nearby would bring his high-powered craft and put it in the lake. It was impressive with its throbbing engine, shining chrome headers, and luxurious interior. But to the skiers and everyone living near the water, he was a definite menace. Seemingly he thrived on racing around the lake churning up the placid water and, in general, shattering the relative calm of the surroundings.

One particular Sunday his small son and another male companion accompanied him out to the lake. Soon he had the throttle wide open, and the trio enthusiastically enjoyed the thrill of power and speed. Then it happened. The father made a sharp turn to the right just as his small son stood to his feet. The centrifugal force catapulted the little boy over the side. The father knew his friend was right behind him and could handle the boat, so he jumped over the other side of the boat, instinctively wanting to rescue his son. The friend, however, did not realize what was happening. He had seen the boy go over one side of the boat and the father leap over the other. Instantly he concluded something was wrong and everyone was abandoning ship, so . . . you

EVERYBODY'S DOING IT!

guessed it! Over the side he went, leaving the unoccupied boat to career around the lake.

Some minutes later, with the help of another boat and a ski rope, the owner managed to bring the driverless craft under control, not only to his relief but also that of the other skiers and boaters on the lake. In retrospect, they can look back with some degree of humor at the time that they were nearly victims of peer pressure.

Victims of Peer Pressure

Such experiences don't happen only to boat enthusiasts in Michigan. Let me tell you about what happened to a friend of mine.

As a boy he noticed a most disturbing fact. His beloved dog had a long shaggy tail, which is, of course, OK—except that all the other boys' dogs in the neighborhood had short tails. The more he thought about the fact, the more it disturbed him. Finally one day when his parents had gone to town he decided to remedy the situation.

Calling his unsuspecting mutt into the kitchen, he lifted him up on the counter. As he stroked his head with one hand, he reached for the meat cleaver with the other. With one swift blow he made his dog like all the other dogs in the neighborhood. The poor animal went yelping off into the woods, not at all impressed by the fact that his master had really thought he had only his pet's best interests in mind. For now he, too, had become a victim of peer pressure.

Now, while this was not a serious atrocity with long-lasting effects (although the pooch might have vigorously debated that at the time), history offers us many more blatant examples. One of the classic incidents used to illustrate "group think," a form of peer pressure, was what happened to the famous John F. Kennedy advisory brain trust.

EVERYBODY'S DOING IT!

A number of high-level government officials began to formulate a plan for invading Cuba. In retrospect, they admitted that not one of them ever challenged the concept. How could they be wrong? They were all in agreement. And so they started planning the now-infamous Bay of Pigs invasion. It was a total disaster with serious consequences and, yes, victims. And, in a sense, all Americans were victims of this great embarrassment to America's credibility —all because not one adviser challenged the plans of the group.

Selecting Your Friends

One more illustration to prove the point—this time a bit more scientific but equally impressive. An American psychologist conducted an amazing study. She informed ten individuals that she was about to hold up a placard with three different-sized lines on it. They were to raise their hands when she pointed to what they perceived as the longest line. Simple enough. What she didn't say, however, was that she had previously told nine of the group that they should raise their hands when she pointed to the medium-sized line to see what the tenth person would do.

After repeating the instructions, she held up the placard and pointed to the shortest line. No one raised his hand. Then she advanced to the medium-sized line, and nine people raised their hands. The tenth person looked at the placard, next at the nine upraised hands, then back to the card, and what do you suppose he did? You guessed it! Sheepishly he put up his hand. The psychologist repeated her experiment with other groups, and 75 percent of the time the participants did not have the internal fortitude to stand up for something they believed was right—even though it was an issue with no more implications than the significance of the length of a line!

EVERYBODY'S DOING IT!

Well, fortunately, that was not the end of the study. The psychologist then repeated the experiment with different groups of individuals but made the ratio eight to two rather than the previous nine to one. What do you suppose happened? The percentage of those who would now stand up for what they knew was right increased significantly. Why? The answer is obvious. It is inherently easier to do what's right if others around you are doing the same thing.

Resisting Negative Peer Pressure

That is one of the most important principles in successfully combating negative peer pressure. Let's apply this fact on a spiritual level. If you are serious about developing a relationship with Jesus Christ you'll choose friends who are friends of Jesus. For example, your choice of school friends is tremendously important. Many times, as a Christian, you may not feel comfortable with a group's choice of type or place of activity. But if you have one other close friend who sees things as you do, it will be infinitely easier to do what is right.

Ultimately, you should carry that principle into the selection of a life partner. If that "special someone" has the same goals, desires, and ambitions in life and is serious about his/her relationship with God, then that person will have a tremendously positive influence on you and your home.

"But," someone says, "my friends aren't Christians, and it doesn't bother me. Besides, look how many opportunities I have to witness!" Unless you are a stronger person than the old patriarch Enoch, you had better watch out! You're on shaky ground.

Genesis tells us that after Enoch became the father of Methuselah, he "walked with God . . . three hundred years" (Gen. 5:22). The birth of his child caused him to see life in a new perspective, and he shifted his association from a degenerating world to God Himself. That relationship led the patriarch to increasingly reject the negative aspects of the pre-Flood society. One cannot walk with God and those hostile to His ways at the same time.

If you seriously want to walk with God, a regular association with those whose influence is negative is one luxury you might not be able to afford. To mingle with them will only destroy any positive transformation God has made in you. The Bible talks of being *in* the world but not *of* it. We live in this world, but we don't let it rule us.

One Christian writer has declared, "The followers of Christ are to separate themselves from sinners [referring to those who do not profess Christ], choosing their society only when there is opportunity to do them good. We cannot be too decided in shunning the company of those who exert an influence to draw us away from God. While we pray, 'Lead us not into temptation,' we are to shun temptation, so far as possible."

Stay Off the Plain of Dura

Let's look at a familiar story—that of Shadrach, Meshach, and Abednego. Has it ever occurred to you to wonder why they were there at the dedication services for an image anyway? Certainly they weren't caught off guard. That golden monument to the greatness of Babylon had been under construction for months. People of that culture and time would naturally expect to have to bow down and worship it.

This brings us to the second point in successfully withstanding peer pressure. (The three young Israelites did at least have one another, so they had that working for them.) Most teenage and young adult Christians should never allow themselves to get on the plain of Dura in the

EVERYBODY'S DOING IT!

first place. What do I mean? Let me explain.

Let's suppose you're with a carload of friends on a Saturday night, and they decide to go to a place of entertainment that you feel is not acceptable. You argue with yourself all the way there as to whether or not you should go in. When they drive up to the entrance, what are the chances of you risking your popularity and taking a martyr's stand by saying that you won't go inside with them?

Well, I'd like to think that as a committed Christian you would unbendingly take that stand. But the earlier illustrations, along with practical experience, tell me that unless you're one of a small minority you'll keep your mouth shut and go on in—feeling you can deal with your conscience later. Right?

Where, then, should you have taken your stand for right? At the entrance? No. That's too late. The time was when you were deciding whether or not to spend the evening with those friends in the first place, realizing full well that they could possibly end up doing something of which you could not approve.

That's what I mean by not getting on the plain of Dura in the first place. Many a conflict is lost in the selection of the battleground rather than in the battle itself. And the same is true of spiritual warfare. When we pray, "Lead us not into temptation," but then carelessly set ourselves up for defeat, we make a mockery of the Lord's Prayer.

So the second key to combating peer pressure successfully is to remember that it's not only the battle that is important but also the battleground. By not allowing yourself to give the devil the unfair advantage, you can avoid many defeats.

EVERYBODY'S DOING IT!

One Plus One = Majority

So why were Shadrach, Meshach, and Abednego present at the dedication of the image? Curiosity? No! Wanting to make a spectacle of themselves? Hardly! Self-chosen martyrs? Again the answer is enthusiastically No!

If you look up the story again, you will find that they had come there in response to the king's decree. It was not by default or because they hadn't considered the consequences. They didn't enjoy the prospect of being a spectacle any more than you or I would, and certainly did not welcome the idea of being a living torch! They had thought it through well. Having prayed and fasted, they fully realized that it would be a trial of their faith that could realistically cost them their lives. Thus they had no other choice. But when the inevitable happened, they could call on Heaven's power because they had developed a daily personal relationship.

Many Christians today will find themselves forced to stand up for what they believe. No prior choices will alter that fact. The devil will at times overrule and put us to the test. Those are the facts of life in our world. It always has been that way, and it always will be—till we get to heaven.

But then, as Paul said: "Having done all, to stand" (Eph. 6:13). In other words, choose your associates carefully. Don't put yourself on the devil's ground; but when the test comes, meet it with confidence. Develop a strong devotional life of prayer and Bible study. Then the story of the three Hebrew youth can be an encouragement to you. Daniel gave a vivid spiritual lesson way back then to encourage us now, especially should we ever face persecution for our faith.

God demonstrated an important lesson through that

EVERYBODY'S DOING IT!

story of His three committed followers, those young men willing to stand for right against incredible odds. And when the inevitable tests come He will be with us. Oh, He won't always visibly walk with us in our fiery temptations. No, but He is there just as certainly. And then you and He become a majority. That's all that counts.

Sitting in a Lobster Pot

A recent survey asked what it is like to be young today. One responded, "Like being a lobster in a boiling pot." It is tough to be a young adult Christian today, no question about it!

I suspect, however, that that teenager didn't realize the full truth of what he said. You see, if you're from New England where eating lobster is a big thing, that statement has more significance because you don't kill and then cook the lobster. Rather, it is alive when you put it into a pot. Then, as the water slowly begins to heat, the lobster becomes used to his condition. Finally, he is actually cooked alive! More serious is the parallel of what happens to many Christians who likewise slowly allow themselves to adjust to the world around them. And it can happen so innocently and yet insidiously—by reading, watching, listening, and general leisure-time entertainment.

That's what the book to the Romans was addressing when Paul stated, "Do not be conformed to this world but be transformed" (Rom. 12:2, RSV). Or as the Phillips version puts it: "Don't let the world around you squeeze you into its own mould."

Longfellow wrote, "In this world a man must either be anvil or hammer," molding his surroundings or being molded by others. You are either a thermostat or a thermometer, setting the temperature of your surroundings or merely reflecting the hot and cold of those around you.

EVERYBODY'S DOING IT!

Down through the ages God's true people have had to stand up to peer pressure. Look at the story of Noah, one of the darkest periods of earth's history.

For 120 long years he and his three sons withstood incredible ridicule. They built that monstrous ship on dry land in full view of the scoffing multitude. Not only did their lifestyle vividly contrast with that of the majority, but the intellectuals and the philosophers of the day ridiculed their simple beliefs as being foolhardy. Eight people against the world. Yet the Bible solemnly warns, "As it was in the days of Noah, so will it be in the days of the Son of man" (Luke 17:26, RSV).

Someone has said that if you want to lead the orchestra you must be willing to turn your back on the crowd. Are you ready to make that kind of commitment? But to do that, you have to determine that by God's grace you're going to follow the three principles of successfully standing up against the majority.

First, carefully choose your friends. Second, determine not to give the devil the advantage by intentionally getting on his battleground. And finally, develop a relationship with Jesus Christ through a devotional life that calls on the resources of Heaven's unlimited power. And then it won't really matter what everybody else is doing!